PARABLE BEACH

poems by

PADDY MCCALLUM

Porcepic Books
an imprint of

Beach Holme Publishing
Vancouver

This book is published by Beach Holme Publishing, 226–2040 West 12th Avenue, Vancouver, B.C. V6J 2G2. This is a Porcepic Book.

The publisher gratefully acknowledges the financial support of the Canada Council for the Arts and of the British Columbia Arts Council. The publisher also acknowledges the financial assistance received from the Government of Canada through the Book Publishing Industry Development Program (BPIDP) for its publishing activities.

The Canada Council | Le Conseil des Arts
for the Arts | du Canada

BRITISH
COLUMBIA
ARTS COUNCIL
Supported by the Province of British Columbia

Editor: Michael Carroll
Production and Design: Jen Hamilton
Cover Art: *Beach at Savary Island, B.C.* by E. J. Hughes, 1952. 20" x 24", oil on canvas. Used with the permission of the artist. Photograph courtesy of the National Gallery of Canada
Author Photograph: Doug Biden

Printed and bound in Canada by Marc Veilleux Imprimeur

Canadian Cataloguing in Publication Data

McCallum, Paddy.
  Parable Beach

  "A Porcepic book."
  Poems.
  ISBN 0-88878-412-0

  I. Title.
PS8575.C3787P37 2000   C811'.6   C00-910658-8
PR9199.3.M42365P37 2000

For Jo and Emily

You have led me from my bondage and set me free
by all those roads, by all those loving means
that lay within your power and charity

—Dante, *Paradiso*, Canto XXXI

CONTENTS

ACKNOWLEDGEMENTS

Some of these poems were originally published in the following journals and magazines:

The Antigonish Review: "In Your Version of Your Brother's Death"

Canadian Literature: "Gifts," "The Lost Son," "The Poetry of George Jehoshaphat Mountain (1789–1863)," "Slumber Music," and "Saturday Night Reading, 1971"

The Dalhousie Review: "River of the Red Fish"

Descant: "The Badger," "The Arsonist," and "Floats"

Event: "Letter from Moscow"

The Fiddlehead: "Luther" and "The World of the Hippo"

Grain: "Orfeo"

The Malahat Review: "Low Tide at Oyster Bay," "Gargoyle Song," and "Red Tide"

The New Quarterly: "Reeds for Gwendolyn MacEwen"

Prism international: "Transfusion"

Quarry: "Parable Beach," "Benjamin West," and "Thomas Scott"

Queen's Quarterly: "Witness" and "The Pioneer Graveyard at Nicola Lake"

Wascana Review: "A Line Drawing, a Coast Unseen"

"Marsh Lament" from *Captivity Voyage* as well as "Passage" and "Sentences for a White Church" from *The Poems of Emily Montague* were first published in *Canadian Literature*.

A limited-edition broadside of "Transfusion" was published by Nemo Press, Comox, British Columbia, 1989.

Poetry
Unearths from among the speechless dead

Lazarus mystified, common man
of death.

—Geoffrey Hill, *History as Poetry*

PART I

GIFTS

Our gifts litter the years behind us
and go bearing our own concerns.
One Christmas
you were reading translations from the Chinese
and your gift came wrapped
in the simplicity of stone.

I carried that heavy image all spring
until your birthday came
and five mysteries broke into your house.
You never forgave me. Even now
all you send are poems
wrapped in burning paper.

This is to let you know my gift is coming.

Prepare yourself for a thousand novels
set at the dawn of time.
They describe how shelves were invented
to hold the artifacts of
misunderstanding. And how each year
the characters extend their home.

A LINE DRAWING, A COAST UNSEEN

Seen on the wall in certain
light it is nothing like her face.
She has glanced away and become
a crude map, an island where her hair falls,
grows over centuries into coral sea.
Her mouth spews endless varieties
of fishes and the wildlife in her eyes
are shy, gathering there at evening
to re-create visions from the Peaceable
Kingdom before the dark brow unleashes
dreams of savaged deer on the hill.

Knowing I would never leave, she threw the map
laughingly in my lap and walked away.
And I have spent small fortunes outfitting
ships and lost whole crews on reefs no sailor
careful of the sea comes near. Alone
I turn out the light to find her lying there.
Sheets twist and billow in moonlight.
Gold runs in the warm shallow of her thigh.

In Your Version of Your Brother's Death

That day you cursed the rule of eternity
into which we all fall, you, too, fell.
I couldn't say this ten years later. I'm
not even sure I can say it today
when two bodies singing earthward still fall
clutching madly at the summer sky. Dying
happens much too early for us all.
Fear of the broken rope, fear of the stones,
fear of the unresponded forest cry. No
ecclesia breaking into praise, invoking
purpose in the tongues of faith, no
history, poetry, swords, and fire, nothing
we inherit prepares us for the sight
of death alone standing with us when we break.

Reeds for Gwendolyn MacEwen

The desert wind is elegy
when utterance fails passion.
Men will cry for you at last and you
will write their limited bodies over
again, directing their caravans
down arteries to markets by the sea

where they will purchase you. Standing white
before the harbour mouth, attending waterfowl
beaten by autumn flight, they
will open you. Perennial reeds will break
and drift and will forever carry you
into snow beds and flower beds and beds wet
with anger.
        Some will speak
the flat discourse of history, others will weave
baskets for your jewellery, and not a few
will rise beneath your better breath to song.

LOW TIDE AT OYSTER BAY

The eyes in a time of dying
grind silent air into grey dust. I awoke
in someone else's bed, stood near a window
and could not speak. For an hour
I watched a heron motionless on a rock
watching the restless fish watch.
I thought of nothing except his wings
tucked tight, but I knew
they were wider than branches,
shadowing the shift of the sea's loll.

I shouldn't sit so still.
Make breakfast, chop wood, listen to the radio,
but I wait for the shape of a shadow
on the wind, waiting
for a sudden eclipse of the sun
that pulls the sea in.

LETTER FROM MOSCOW

Snowflakes are falling on the path that runs
past the fountain where your regiments
came and went. It has never been so cold.
History has lain down in the snow.
I part the bushes above its burrow
to find my sleeping soldiers
wrapped around their ancient weapons.
I hear your black boots advance upon the hill
their slow tread crushing all
memories of the harvest into ghettos, drills
and gun emplacements. I loved you
on your tall horse that autumn, but then
you rode back across the border
with your blue hands, black lips, defeat
at my tenacity slowing you to a crawl.
I dream of you now at balls and parties
raising your glass to the will of the enemy.
It's a sure thing you have forgotten me
and only remember the bright expanse
of my body under candlelight; and the snow,
the snow over pages of memoirs, those
you read now, live in, and die.

THE LOST SON

Often
when I'm lonely for my son
I go out among the wet flowers
and paw the muddy grass
and taste its sulphur.

Or I climb the beach from
tower to tower
but he is gone, perhaps
he is gone into
water. My toes
kick the salt-packed
logs set free from boom
and blade and fire. They
are history. Memory
is a child.

And when I find my son
and lift him in my mouth
and lay him in his mother's lap
am I not then free?

They devour each other
and gaze at me.

I go outside for dusk
for quiet.

The mule deer vanish
with apples to the forest.

River of the Red Fish

Now, after all this time, I return to you.

Forgive me for forgetting the languages
you taught me. My banks are flooded
every season with indifference.

My boat has found no pilings safe as yours.
There is nowhere to hide, no cool sand
beneath no bridge, beside no forest
ripe with the sweet smell of marsh cabbage
blooming always in late summer.

I have lost no shoes swimming
when I should have been at school.
No mouth has entranced me as yours does
when you meet the Fraser. No bones
are buried deeper in me than those
of a tribe lost forever.

Nothing terrifies like you in January.

No dogs cross the water behind me
carrying all I need to survive.

I'm not even sure I survive
without you. Certainly I have not
found timber strong enough
to navigate you. It is my shame
that long ago I gave up searching.

Your banks consume me now to the waist.

In thirty years
my heart will emerge
from the mud like an eel
to drink with you.

Gargoyle Song

All around me there are streets leading
away from the piazza. And down each street
there is someone walking away from me.
There is a woman with her hair cut
straight across her forehead. There is a man
carrying a warrior mask he brought from America.
There is a friend who just forsook the one
person who would never forsake him.
And there is some light left in the piazza
but no wind. It's blood-warm on the fountain.
I close my eyes. The taps push on.
Goldfish fall from my mouth, and start to swim.

PARABLE BEACH

This morning eats at colour like a snake
taking it whole. I breakfasted
at a small café I know
where men in overalls rummage in the paper
and the seasmell blows in
from the opening opening door.

On five miles of beach I am
a single tourist. Walking,
my loins heavy with bacon
and my legs like the posts
beneath abandoned shacks of
fishermen who lost direction

just as if their boats had busted up
in coves too far from help

the fishing ended.
                    Cormorants pick at seawhips
with eyes like tax officials, while
a real-estate agent with a tape measure
casts it from house to house.

What of the story shut tight as an oyster
in the guts of men too old
to say they've failed? Or the sea
them?

On land half-covered by water
in water grey as sand
nameless tiny fish are trapped
and seastars move into the deep receding centre
slowly slowly knowing one shift of cloud
brings out the searing killing sun.

PART II

THE ARSONIST

Long after the police gave up their search
and the papers stopped asking why of
former analysts and the one girlfriend
who really knew him married and moved
to Hamilton carrying what may have been his child
he retired.

          At the age of thirty-one with
twenty-three decrepit warehouses to his credit
he trusted himself to live by candlelight
telling stories till all hours of
the Two Flames: the one without and
the one within, the fire that made the news
and the one that burned for days
alone with him, until with perfect
pitch the flames grew softer and he wept
terrible hot ice steaming around him.

His sense of narrative was weak, but he knew
enough of rags and how to place them. Such
care his mother said he could have been
an artist. But his was the greater calling.
In his mind he delivered lectures detailing
how his negatives drew, for an instant,
attention to forgotten buildings leaving
holes in abandoned neighbourhoods that were
holes in the dying city.

At this point he lit
six candles and slept among them. In dream
he saw the party dresses, wild gestures, and
birthday hats: laughter tipped by a napkin
into flame.

THE WORLD OF THE HIPPO

Sometimes when I'm cleaning fingerprints
or vacuuming cobwebs from the corners
of the sky he lumbers by, just an inch
above my head and I could push an opening
no larger than a hole in the sky
to fall through and find myself
in the African dawn avoiding
his big soft hoof.

                    His determination
would be as mysterious as an
after-dinner snooze; for he, and the mighty
working of his jaws are the Earth's
own image when it tires of standing still.

Tufts of dust kick up like the steam
from hot ice. His great nose has become
our compass as we seek nonheat or fall
into a deadly fly-clogged dream too far
from mud. Where I once trotted I now walk
and listen and learn from him all things
known in the predawn: that occasionally
there is sex but always there is water;

that a thousand acres of ripened grass
are no bigger than a pond; that one can be fooled
by memories of mountain lakes
larger than the sky for the sky
is the clarity of evil and its heart
a scalding mouth that vomits flies.

                                        This

he left me with at the riverside
before he shattered reeds to enter
the cool truth and float there, a grey stone where
no stones are, an island the flies sail to.

SATURDAY NIGHT READING, 1971

for Earle Birney

A draft of wind across the campus light,
perhaps the thousand drafts
of late October bringing scent of berries
from the throat of the mountain bear.

I was hiding. It is wise to hide from bears
for to come upon one in late October
even in hope of hearing his song
(these bears sing of elsewhere)
is to grunt or run.

I stood still, hiding.

I watched the fur of the bear turn white.
I heard the voice of the bear make peculiar
laughter, and was terrified.

The beautiful eyes of the bear
glowed moraine as they fell upon me.
I would never leave these woods
nor the path so heavy with frost.

The bear winked.

In a bear-blink he caught me. His head
cocked thoughtfully, "Hey there,"
he sang, "comin' in?" and my spine
bent like a porcupine and my paws
knew the world around me.

Sing? I would dig if I could not sing
in his green woods exploding.

RED TIDE

I answered the back door late one night
to find the otter standing there.
His salty breath still stank of fish.

I don't know why I followed him,
ran, in fact, down trails to the beach.
Just the two of us, lonely and cold,
following step by step the tide.

Three feet from the awesome drop-off
the dissolving feathers of dead gulls
covered me, stuck to me
as I fell forward into the black sea.

And all at once I knew the territory,
the inverted weeds, the oyster clock.
I thought of my friends as I walked,
of acrimony, jealousy, of St. Paul,
his mental maps, his memory.
I thought of my wife's body
rolling over and over in her white sheet.
I felt her hair lolling into a brown wreath
while I knelt at the foot of a coral mountain.

Each small disease of the water
inhabited me with love. Above
the otter watched the old sun surface
while my dark red world of clay arose.

My arms embraced beneath the bashful stone.
My legs flicked their tails and were gone.
I tried to speak but my tongue had grown.
How its eel-eyes shone!

My hair washed strand by strand
onto the coast of Oregon. And my wife
gone, rose from her slow bed.
She closed her eyes against the dawn
to breathe me, finally, purely, in.

THE DEAD ONE

None of us knew the dead one's name
or how to read the message: a grammar
of shirtsleeves and boots on the beach
and near the water underwear bore
testament to his vulnerability.

Nothing in his cold eyes heard us calling.

At knee-deep some found money
and around our knees his watch.

Closer still to our throats we opened
our silent mouths to waves,
submerging, if necessary (and it was)
to speak in hypothermic tongues with him

and learn well the accident of breath
all pressure kicks, uselessly,
against the opposing heart.

Though time taught us to live on coral
and eat what the sharks did not
our eyes burned for news of him.

The search seemed systematic: keels provided
direction; hooks and line, protection.

Occasionally, vast-bellied boats spun
above us, their hum furnishing memories
of sky and sun.
                    But
we no longer paused to listen.
Our quest consumed its own desired end.
Reefs became mazes we thrived in, watching
each other clutch fingernail clippings
or gurgle approvingly at scraps of skin.

It was pitiful; so contempt began
and our search ended with each other.

At first we satisfied our need
with bruises and scratches from stone.
Later on we learned to use our teeth.

Now the ocean reddens daily
and every hand like the original hand floats free.

ORFEO

Today in the lonely woods
I met two falling friends in love.
They lay with me between them
and all that separated their mouths
was old hair and old feeling.

My love was old before I met her.
She died two years older than I.
Each day I sing of her mouth
and of her hair falling out.
She steps from the earth to thank me.

I shouldn't sing this song of burls,
a song it's wrong even to remember.
"End your exile," she whispers, "meet my father."
It's cold at night. Beasts howl.
Her white voice cries of burning in the east.

FLOATS

For thirty years I listened patiently
to stories told by those who travelled
the long way round the island. They spoke
of houses built from whale teeth,
of ribs fencing the beach and the screams
of winged women drowning above the sea.
They spoke of expectation as of food
and chanted out in rhythms meant to capture
the long-enforced bobbing of the floats
names of ships and cities never seen.

They were not living in my imagination
so I poured them cups of tea until,
drugged by their endlessly imitated surf,
they wrapped their arms around me
and I travelled with them.

As first they nearly suffocated me.
All I could do was lie and watch the treetops
folding open. I cried from terror
at the blue sky and fevered at the density
of starlight. And all the while
their chanting broke stones in my head
and their feet pounded pounded pounded
on the road like a truck. So many days
I became Motion. I asked for nothing
but the wind, so to keep me alive at night
they passed me among them or left me
to wander well-protected in fields.

Then, on the fifth day after leaving
the last gas station, we passed a million
trees running in the opposite direction.
A terrible roaring broke their trunks
and their boughs groped forward blindly.
My bowels streamed down my legs breeding
tidal pools. I knelt among companions
who coughed up sandstars and watched while others,
bound in kelp, waited for the tide to feed them.

And here and there, tossed in surf,
the strange floats beckoned.

My finger scratched at sand as if to live
was to touch them. To my eyes, at first,
they were nothing: crudely coloured glass
balls wrapped in bits of twine, but slowly
my eyes swam there. I floated bluer
than deepest ocean with the twine
tightening around my mouth. Bracing,
I pulled my legs against my chest
and hugged my knees and pushed my face
deeper and deeper into my crotch shaking
all the while in the pure white turbulence
of broken waves.
                Soon, only my single
blue eye remained, wrapped in bits of hair.
What I had forgotten of myself floated
elsewhere carrying driftwood with it.

The sea is only a moment of light
and I have lived for three days in the stomach
of a whale and a thousand years in
Arctic ice. Currently I dwell on rocks
and watch the great sea turtles mate.

WITNESS

You are strolling at dusk with a woman by your side
and she's gone. Suddenly
you're walking with a group
of tourists dressed in pink.

Some have dogs or carry umbrellas.
Others wear baseball caps.
They are heading to the beach
to watch the last horizon.

One of them says, trying to be helpful,
"When you open your eyes in eternity
the first thing you'll see
will be the face of God."

You make every effort to turn away
but there is something compelling in
their pink journey. Only they
have entered the process
of turning slowly into clouds.

On the beach the man at the table
has a thousand copies of the same book
open to a thousand pages.
"Here is the story of science and faith.
Here is the Warrior Version. Look, the Song of Love.
Over here, the Gospel of Death."

The words of each volume are printed on glass.
They overflow with history, pornography
and math. The steady drip
of language onto sand
reminds you of rain in another country.

Your friends play volleyball or sing to themselves.
They walk the beach or forget your name.
No one else approaches the table.
They made their choices long ago.

At sunset they quietly disrobe.
You fear your scars and missing parts
the organs and extremities bobbing
out to sea. O yes
you are relieved of the burden of beauty.

Your chest rattles into the tide.
Clouds couple and dissipate.

Inside, the ancestral water
of the body is warm and sweet.

TRANSFUSION

The Cosmic Dancer, declares Nietzsche,
does not rest heavily in a single spot...

1

If this is God's mouth,
if we writhe in it,
if there is language
in acres of silt
and pylons are teeth
that the wind corrodes,
teasing fricatives
when the river drops,
then I was swimming
in the blood of His heart.

2

These things happened
here, do happen now:
rivers merge, their flight
into perfect sea
begun; trees unleash
from flood-broken banks,
into that expanse
of pure mind, sand grains
whirling like black stars,
wings like ashes of sun.

3

When, sighting a hawk,
his fall a claw, his
fall a fingernail,
he fell an instant
out of sight, behind
or in tall grass, fell
beyond the river,
did you hear nothing?
Not even when sight
once more set waves lapping

4

throughout the air
until it seemed hawks
swooped everywhere.
Then lightening the shape
of white cattle bones
and chunks of bank fell
into the river.
Just that, nothing more,
but that it happened
here—water where wings beat.

5

O, I could have fear.
It's not intention
though, not even will
shapes the current so.
Whoever bends earth
is earth, no less. Was
it willful to say
that God forms water
in His mouth to speak?
Hands dip likewise to drink.

6

Now an otter swims
whiskered in winter,
shameless bold tenant
of the underpier.
In his mouth the fish
breaks free, out of nets
wide as a river.
Above his dock, boughs
catch feathers. Tears, His, freeze.

The Badger

I

Two hunters cross a soggy field.

The one in the foreground drags
his kill, leaving a trail
for the one who follows.

                          Do not
wait for them to reach you.

Go out ahead and greet them, carry
a rock or stick (this to
let them know your
hands are larger now)

                             offer them
shelter, clean clothes.

In the morning when they wake
they must not find you.

II

Moving north by certain
backroads, you will have heard
by now that I am wanted.

They say those hunters found
the old girl's carcass. They say
everything on the farm was dead.

She lived there too long.

Your leather satchel I
carefully buried, filled with
stones (clumsily) and dirt.

I am certain you can walk freely
in the streets today.

III

Maps are no defence
against a night this black.

Calculating the odds
I waited five weeks beside this road
for one crushed badger

and made proper magic with its eyes.

Now I've taken to ditches
with my nose
                              and see
how it is for the outcast in this world.

Destroy any messages for me:
I have become unapproachable.

IV

The old bitch was true,
only the eyes are real.

But from *here* descent is rapid.

I should have killed a bear or cougar.

Coward. Coward.

V

Nightmare: You are an infant
(pick your species) asleep
in a low cradle by moonlight.

Everything is silent.

Then foliage rustles in no wind,
twigs crack beneath soft feet.
(Can you hear
what it means to be awake and hungry?)

Above you two
growling pupils blacker than night

and a mouth full of blind
teeth like maggots

                          their insistent
                          heat

then suddenly bumping whipped by branches
glimpsing a dark hole near an old stump.

Then you know you'll never waken.

VI

By now I am renowned in the forest,
even wolves avoid me.

                    You too
may have heard news of me, such like:

*There's a vicious old badger, big as a man, on the hill
with a white badge on his forehead brighter than a diamond.
He kills for the love of it. At night you can hear the
shrieks of animal young. This one's so bold he raids our
chickens and tears out the eyes of dogs!*

I've kept those eyes
deep in my burrow:

A large black dog might bay by your window
wearing on his forehead a bright white beacon.

Feed him.

VII

Sleep is murdered. Each day
packs of hunters pass my den
with hounds toward the river
where they sniffle for badger
and snarl at robins.

I'll move my burrow tomorrow.

VIII

They cornered me
snooting through a log near dawn.

The dogs are sporting
and I feel compelled
to dart out at them and claw.

My eyes are torn
and I've become all smell:

much boot leather and gunpowder
behind the odour of dog, beyond that
the wide river and my new burrow
with its moist earth and dusting log
near a matting of crushed fern.

Deep piss and bird droppings
linger in the air.

Rainwater gathers in pools
on the forest floor.

Wake me. Wake me. The sun is here.
Home is where we die. Or where we are.

Or who we were. Or what.

IX

Two hunters cross a soggy field.

The one in the foreground drags
his kill, making a trail
for the one who follows.
                      Do not
wait for them to reach you.

Go out ahead and bring them clothing,
lead their dogs to the kennel.

Wash them, feed them,
bring fresh bedding,
see that they sleep near a window.

Climb the hill by moonglow,
find my eyes in blood by the burrow:

Roll them in spittle, shake them thrice.

Nothing and no one that came must go.

PART III

FROM *THE POEMS OF EMILY MONTAGUE*

With such spirit such a mind as hers must love.

—Frances Brooke

The History of Emily Montague (1769)

You stand behind these wanting words
and speak them as you would your own.
Fanciful friend, we are alone.
There are no voices 'cept this one
and it is silent till you come
to close upon me with your tongue.

—E.M.

Evening Prayer

Now at the hours of Sext and None
I wait for thee with an open palm
and hammer there with point'd finger
harden'd metal far too rare
for skin, too sharp for love.

Some might push my hand away
and cry, *Enough! What trick is this?*
Alone, you stand beside me. O take us
home, Crucify'd Lord. You, Dew,
cool these nails that drive me.

The Cut

You did not know when my flesh first ripp'd
a rune-shaped heart upon your fingertip,
ashamed to be so separate
and make you think—O certainly not!—

there is some stranger lives in her blood

so much so you thrust the finger
to cleanse (by deluge?) that reservoir—
the Two in the One, the Infinite—
the first perhaps, and final Cut.

So like you then to wander from my room
into your darkening world alone
original, naked, without stain,
Adam's child holding his lover's pain.

Creation

In the beginning I was parchment
until you came and fold'd me gently
and cover'd me with thought. Yes,
too pale for you from the start
I earn'd my darkness kiss by touch
upon the yellowing raiment toss'd
from desk to rug and finely embrac'd.

You, who have the world outraced, control
New Heaven if you would New Earth
and place my trickl'd body at the heart
each line to guide some new man's way
into perpetual night. I will stay,
the continent's morning light, awash
in utterance from this paper trail

leading thought by thought to some
New World, not mine. Forgive my love
too pale. My story is trope, icon, shrine.
You, who have made this body's design
will read this skin at some New Dawn.
By then the pale little girl will be gone
who canter'd pretty in the morning sun.

Passage

Now, here is a story

A man gazes through a high window at
the awesome splendour of the world.

Well, here I am, he recalls.
And there it is.

His right hand reaches up into the light.

His left hand grips his lover
in a small spoil of earth.

To E.R.

I have never thought of me, it's you I see
where the road splits all ways and light broods
over the river, as barges do
and ferries, and you
bringing tales of wild courtship
in the shaming woods—
(O shame that would correct me!)

Kingdom come in carts, in oxen
crying out against the mud. I cannot
think of me or know this urgency
as freedom—would you have me squat
in camp smoke, my skin
slick with fat?—here in prosody
my hair is loos'd, your hands move in.

Somewhere in these tales of Paradise
are Character and Plot, the temptation
to flourish in the Fall, to see
how the paths of love come sublimely
to rock or ice. This letter is us
prostrate—my body's history
scold to a fallen nation.

A Locket

Your silent image fills the room.
The paint says nothing, nor the frame
for all its gilt a muted thing.
You come and go and I remain
like desire—desire though absent
still desire—merely to love again.
I close this part of you that owns
the past, the rings and precious stones
surround a face without a story.
What was it that you wrote to tell me?
My hand must hold what the tale meant.
Forgive conceit: I'll keep the face
at least it stays to take embrace.

Sentences for a White Church

White church even to speak of perfection
is to fill the mouth with soil.

White church who restores *you*
when graves break open like packing crates?

Your stones in a passing thought
become stones.

My fingers linger down the face of an angel.
Tears collect beneath my nails.

I read your hymnal with my one blind eye.

White church the arms
of winter grass the immigrant grass
shame me O liar.

Here is a haven for the dreams of a clown
and flaming stairs for the frostbitten girl
who loves you white

church but neither of us
is coming in.

Unseen

...leave Canada to those whose duty confines them here,
or whose interest it is to remain unseen.

That we should have stumbled in such
fecund ground and fear the success
we're born to, never growing
beyond the having of excuses
and such fine manners.

These open, green, and fertile borders,
all the naiveté of Nature
let loose, untend'd—to be
unseen in a land of wonders
silences me, another rodent in another tree
who keeps on chattering
of pursuits and promises.

I am one of those whose dreams complain
of soil and weather, for even you
come upon me like disease
in a child in a world so young
our bones must still be forming
earth, empires, lovers.

Look how my language spins
into the river mouth, a wide red
shadow of silk, wider than the angry
mind of God when He contemplates
chaos and the vanity
of thought.
      Let us be happy
then, those of us invisible
for we alone may probe the future
stem by flower, becoming
shades of the Garden
and the Gardener.

THE POETRY OF GEORGE JEHOSHAPHAT MOUNTAIN (1789–1863)

Forms of the long canoe-hymn. Narratives
of narratives of wild conversion,
though of rivers there was little
he could bring his tired Assembly,
having secured his birchbark poems
to the Mission dock so firmly
he failed to make them hear the heart
of his dog as it swam its nineteenth spring
to greet him. Landscapes
quivered in their eyes Elysian.

So when the ice broke he loaded supplies
and headed west again to preach. Bears
became sheep. The singular state
of the trapper his own soul's fate.

Songs, he said, and the days sang slowly by.

At certain points the river shallowed
redeeming eels from bedrock, trout
like the fallen pieces of sky he lived on.

Deer watched with the eyes of saints
as remnant Huron found protection
in his wet arms, knee-deep. The sun
when they rose was sheer white.

His years stretched stanzaic Missions
along the thirsty riverbanks. Failed epics.
His lines rhapsodic, pure, shorter
than praise, slighter than images,
a glimpse of fields where the richest soil
runs its perfect furrows to the sun.
Songs all evening. Prayers at dawn.
Trails cut by the flames of His gown.

LUTHER

O how I tremble on this lonely oaken
bench where I can hardly kneel.

Woodrot and bug-filled rafters,
and beneath the mantel a fire is burning
warming a hearth that does not welcome
any man, any woman.
                    Sing of His glory,
sing of trembling, sing
of the dust and ashes
                              waiting.

My knees have almost grown
calluses. I yawn
and dream of a woman cold as iron
who laughs and sends me home

and I finger an odd-shaped stone
always waiting in my pocket.

"He is your undoing
as fire consumeth a house"

and I know that I cannot pray in dark cathedrals
and I need to stand alone.

I watch a long cloak sway in the corner
and a white hand
dust the altar

64

as the eastern sun comes shimmering through
the Fifth Station of the Cross
where Christ stumbles again

                     waiting

for this man to kneel and push
with all his might to raise
this bloody, soled thing another mile.

THOMAS SCOTT

Stone is the bread we ate, and stone
the earth we dipped it in

I am. A man
of dirt and daily bread
uncomfortable enough to dream
this life will end.

Up out of the ditch I pulled my men,
for a moment we were bosses,
lady, for a moment I was
ready to make amends
to you, the Company, Snow, etc.

Where, I ask now, have I been led?

When a man asks for work
and none appears
he gets strange ideas in his head

of hatred, compensation, and revenge,
the like of which Riel knows well.

We talked. He stood
mumbling to the guard,
his back to me,
facing an old man with a lamp,

Scott sera execute was all I understood.

Let him ride the plains and whoop;
I've seen it all my life.
From old women whipped on the streets of Dublin
to this piece of dirt
is a step any man could take.

Stone was the mould I ate
when Catholics burned the farms of Donegal,
and snow is the grave I earn
beside a river named like blood,

cursed as a yokel, cursed for my skin,
just as my forefathers faced this shame
in the holds of ships; chattel
washed on the beaches awaiting
whoredom or the field...

Lady! Lady, I am so afraid
of burial half-alive or some
final indignity that finds me kicking
about in the mud like a pig.

Let the men be quick.
                              Let Jesus
cast away this flesh and show
mercy on this man too much afflicted
with the sins of the sin of Pride.

Benjamin West

Rain that whole night through
beat down upon the street like hooves.
I hear that pounding sound
at the edge of prayer
where your needlepoint spins your arm
as if to call me near.
I'm nearer than you know.

Dreams last night of lightning
and white horses. In some corner
far off and black I felt Redemption move
in figures slim and bright.
Or was that earlier, at the play?
My back hurts from that studio chair.
A little brandy and a lot of sleep,
reading old letters, a novel,
some poetry too.
                      These evenings
bend low as a broken man.

Tons of water pour
through gutters and the garden!
Something tosses the clouds,
shakes itself and swirls!
Dark and indistinct though I swear
hands thrust at me from
the edge of Sky.
                      My hands cling to the drapery
and only remember the touch of velvet.

THE PIONEER GRAVEYARD AT NICOLA LAKE

The small fence around your stone
slumps like a cowshed
as death reenters, hammer in hand.

Even in dreams you could not
get through, meeting him
on the road at midnight
or by the sea
or the apple tree.

Some men have minds
like the west, a hard perpetual
tomorrow, they build
the church first
and never enter it.

He stood here, right here
and beat out the words of your name
with the chisel and mallet
his hands had become

to find what outside himself
resembled you

worn granite, folded arms
still protecting, down
this hundred years and more,
still more, your
winter daughter

ten days old.

BIG DOG

from *The Journals of David Thompson* (1810)

A day any man of science should have known
by sextant, mercury, and horizon line,
a day of observation in the land of bear
made by clear advantage of weather,
mosquitoes grown fat under
dispassionate glass, their legs splayed
like sketchings of rivers measured,
reasonably, in quantities of blood.

A day of walking into the misunderstood
but not of talking. Who could stomach that?
Sick children, Piegan guides wary
of waterfalls and Blackfeet, a wife...well,
she'd rather navigate a sturdy hut
and yet, she makes little sound.
Her skirt rustles the hill with prayers.
It is the spoken wind

of a perfect day for spooking horses
driven mad by flies and pack and tilt.
Mine fell, a sack of broken skins, then shot.
Only an old Cree, captive, understood.
"The first horse we ever saw was dead.
He lay on his side with an arrow in his gut
and looked like a stag without horns,
a slave to all, so we called him Big Dog."

I laid the horse under a perfect mat
of reindeer moss, cranberry, and moose scat,
alive again, body unto body: Manito.
Tonight among the pipes I read from *John*
and sketched this leg of our slogging
under such a lamp of Heaven's glow
I could shoot an owl at twenty yards
and run, with Big Dog, a slave to the stars.

SLUMBER MUSIC

Love shall be our Lasting Theme
Love shall Every Soul Inflame
Always Now in Realms Above
Ah, Amen Redeeming Love

—Henry Alline
Hymns and Spiritual Songs (1786)

I

Fallen Nature interposed. Edwards
and Whitefield on comprehending knees.
Days blown from calendars to
cannonaded trees. Shields
of waves, black fire
on the wheeling western plains.
Children wandering deeper
into untended streams.
              Why, Alline,
have you come again?

To urge the Sparks back into Flame.

II

All day the river mouth breathes
brown silt. Jets fall
on twenty centuries of upland spit.
Crows chatter the Arctic wind.

I hear a thump-bash of stump,
turn, and find you,
woodpecker,
feasting on carpenter ants.

A black frock coat, a cap of red,
and talk so long I fall from flight
to drift for flies through honeycombed
continents, caught,
gutted, high on the dock.

III

At large over centuries, criminal gnostic,
you claim some vision of the land
of confluence—the sea off Yarmouth, N.S.,
port of God's great salutation,
stigmata of barrel splinters, rope burn,
backs bared to reflected sun,
salt fingers moving down your spine

and come at intervals, like exultation,
like history, burning up the airwaves
where your sure-fire God of Love
shatters monitors in the chill despair

of a once and tall November dawn.

IV

Love, you said, Love?
But it died kneeling in the wheeling
Rivers of Arcadie where the bone-chilled
Penitents bathed against the Flood
against their Heat against the Sea
while their Hearts broke and the Land
stayed, stupefying, strong.
                    Go on,
the Dead arise the Quick erupt
Volcanic, spreading Red Dreams
of Judgement into that broken Moment
we call—you lead, go on, shout it—

Prayer.

V

Musket breath from Tongueless Redcoats
staked to the trees of Monongahela.
Braddock weeping in his tent at night
for the New World awash in New Light.

Divines tending the unsought call
of William Law in his ear.
                    A Breeze.
A million Bibles hard as Lead loosening
his grip, his
Horse, riderless.

Catalogues and Hymnals. Gulls
feeding fleeing Ships, Flags
caulking the Hold.

VI

I enter wars repeatedly: Dawn
of a thick wet field. So, so many
are crying out behind, in, thickets.

Trees russet with the stench of men.

Jesus God am I the battle

or in the battle
              can
anyone speak
here

singing twenty years away the Mist and Shadow.

VII

Neither the dead nor the living dead.

You praise wakefulness but not the dawn.

Tombs and kingfishers
hunt the shores of mountain lakes.
They are the Missions.

Their doors and windows take to the wind

rising and crying to Heaven.

VIII

Noon, after a thunderstorm.

All the insects of the fallen world
outcast: low and lonely, gasping
from their contest with Sacred Air,
drought, predators everywhere.

I called to them along the beaches
weeping for fear: "Rise up you Armies
and blot out Heaven. The Sun
is but a fellow Victim." For here was pain,
a multitude screaming,
every stone a breathing Shadow,
every electric limb aswarm.

Empires flooded my face
as the Drowned swept from my Wandering Footwork
back to Shore.

I drank of them till I could drink no more.

And sank there, bloated,
my stomach a hive for the Damned,
and their Generations thrive.

IX

Dawn. Love's music
slumbers on her instrument.

You quote *Ephesians*. I rummage my closet
for armour as your troops move
past my window in neat eternal file.
It's been so long since I killed anyone.
My brain failed your experiments
in chemistry. Forgive me.

Forgive me, Scientific God, whose breath
reeks of Nitre. Bytes of Diogenes fall at the feet
of your Prophets. They are idle.
They never left the steps of your Temple.
Their days arrange small accidents of History.

Like preachers.

Like poetry.

X

Ineffable Virus, succulent Witch, haunting
benches, toilets, alleyways.
When You sleep on steam grates
I remain unmoved. When You molest Children
I choke, but it passes.
I resist You, yes, and am troubled for it.

Cloud Your Voice and come as Rain.
Pierce Your Ears, blazen Your hair,
enter my Veins through a thousand shades
of lipstick. Though You undulate
earth, stone, the latest City,
You move this itching part of me
elsewhere only, covered in Legend.

...spoken from salt marshes at our wet feet
through sweet-loam deltas of sleep.

PART IV

CAPTIVITY VOYAGE

from *The Songbook of Pierre-Esprit Radisson*

What hath that Nation done to thee in being so far from
thy Countrey?

30th October, 1653

At 4 o'clock of the evening of the day
of failing courage I found my selfe lost
in a vast clearing of trees

wich made me look hard unto my selfe
and my design for habitation
and the strangenesse of our sojurn here

whereby to save this Life that men so love
they abhor themselves and so sedduce
all those terrores wich they apprehend.

Thus comes a man who cutts still wood
and visiones me as Iroquois. Thus I barter
while his curios wife dreames of wildmen.

But trade is the bed and trade the table
whereon the meals I have eaten lie:
inseks, mudd, and thigh. My fate always

to find mine Selfe in the blood of another
who watches him flee the Fire
leeping the Damned like a white-tailed deere.

The River Ovamasis

At the rising sunne I wake my Brother
telling by signs it is time to goe

but he cries of the reste
that none will stir.

From my heavy head I shake her fingers:
the bracelets and songs
of no escape, no pleaysure.

I rise and goe to the waterside
and walk awhile and dreame.

Here. It is *here*
I will make a world of my selfe
running my naked sword
into the wandering sand

till One come out of the myst
and call to me and showe his way
setting dishes of meat
upon the riverside
stinking and red as me
who crawles to eate (a bear?)
now like a bear.

Marsh Lament

Being come to the lake height
we drague our boats over trembling ground
of castors drowning in great soyles.
Herein grows mosse 2 feet thick
just when you think to goe safe and dry.
Dead water out of one hole
and into another.

Just when you think only madmen can help you
just when you lose half your bodie
and women pass you dry as wood
and you eat the cord
having no use of the bow, where then
is Time Past and Plentynesse
when the poore cry daily?

You, called Gods of the Earth, how
will you make your hole in the snowe?

I, here, shall hold to the mosse
and cast forth sudainly
and goe like the frogg
dragging my green boats after me.

The Portall of St. Peter

After this we came to a remarquable place...

From a banke of Rocks wich signify
the likenesse of the Devil
wild men hurl tobacco
into the Great Portall.

10 heads, foure prisoners, our bellyes
full of the flesh of enemies.
Watch how they burne like holy martyres
and blowe their tydes of ashe
beyond the boystrous Lakehead.

Am I strong enough for all that I say
to eate my fill and fling the rest away?
Name this hole St. Peter
by reason of the beaten Rock

and goe into our Countrey then
dark and ever deeper
and burne men there at leasure
untill the Portall fills, untill
this Stone shatters us all.

Scaffold Marche

I cant say how that houre passed
but the weather was verie faire

me, five men, three women, two childs
replentished Heaven with oure cries

then the Sunne departted
and came the raines O Lorde

to beatt for the Band of Hell

Kyrie

*I, after this finding my selfe somewhat alterd and my bodie more
like a devill than anything else...could not dijest but must sufer
all patiently*

When I close mine eyes I see them still
hanging at the ends of ropes
quarkling like henns

stumps of fingers picking Fire
their stones rolling
through the games of children.

Now and again some water
the mercy of sleep.

Then I awake in a suit of barke
and take my place in the Lightning Forest
and hear my father crie,
"You senseless! Thou lovest not.
 Give him to eate!"

My rootes reech into the earth of Others
drinking the blood of murdered tongues

dry and silent I have no minde
and watch my heart paint the face of a child

and fall at last and rowe
with steeming branches on to Paradice.

Love Explanes All

Whenever I wake from sleep with you
I feel the pain of nails
a brilliance seeping through my skin
my bodie bent like the figur 2
in a rocking crib with animals.

Some times you grab and slapp my face
your words fill my throat with nettels

O blessed Sacraments of Fire
O singing broken by the smell
of frankinsence and spices
the fragrance of oure Bodies
a-rising into light.

At my right one daughter of Christ
beats her head against the post
her bodie reels and totters.
Daggars peerse her side.
Wine runs from lips of marbel.

Love explanes all.

Chanson

Because I did not stop to mourne
the loss of Christes sweete bodie
men ask these days for nothing
and give me miserie

Because I did not stop to mourne
I can no longer walk
and thrust my knees into the bogg
my hands into the rock

Because I did not stop to mourne
Saulteur, Cree, Odawas
pipes of councell rost my arse
sett with precious jewells

Because I did not stop to mourne
animals mounted me
birds transformed my hair
into a bloodie tree

Because I did not stop to mourne
I live now like as God
carefully arranging
the names that I am called

Canto Fermo

...so much as the minstrel might sing at one "fit"

Children you must die
though this Countrey is Beautifull
though you carryed the vessells
that we most need

Pork-a-pick a bout youre heads
garlands like a Crowne—
mariages, alliances
the bones of the dead

a sack upon youre shoulders
in all the world inclosed
Children you must die
though youre faces be not stayned

Gravitie and modestie
youre buff coats on the ground
Children you must die
not with daggar, not alone

New Jerusalem Stone

So hard to breathe. The aire is full
of prayer and lamantation
and boughs a-flame like towers
from the Book of Psalms.

I said, let me show you Ressurection.
Let me show you one burning man
arriving through confession
where too many Rivers meet.

He came to warr through a Golden Gate
that blocks the paths of Peace
with blood and commerce.
Another of God's conundrums.

He has never seen so many tombs
a-rising from Death's defeat
each making so much of tribe and soil
and toil and every Fate

all of it spillt on Hade's grate
a-rising unto this Heaven
or that. Whichever way he lookes
oure painted Pilgrims burne

leggs like willow sticks collapsing
into smoke that was tomorrow.
The bones of historie mixing
stones for the Street of Sorrow.

Among the Risen

I know not if the Soule be large
or wide as the lande wich holds it

but must sit some dayes in wilderness
a palisade of an hundred cabbans
or hollow river a mile in breadth
with twentey boats all waiting.

Perhaps at night it seems to me
that Soule must walk as woman
and lay her lips upon my cheek
and fill my mouth with meat

so I survive and rise to greete
a living visione of that same Soule
chanting the childe in her arms
to saw away my finger.

Heer in the raine that Essens takes
the glowe of a copper isle.
Dry mosse. Calm wynds. A thicke
path beaten by the feet of Man.

Last

Thereafter come many to search for me
and call my name
and thinke me dead longe sinse

for they come on the Third Day
tho I am flown

mother to sister to father to son
searching for any meanes
to end my Voyage

by shallops, ships, fishers, ill
weather Holland to Quebec to
my Wildmen home

In my absens, peace

tho the winde is favourable for us NW
blowing on my fingers
of war and wildernes
the reasons I stay not longe
yet longe

NOTES

The Badger is indebted, in part, to John La Farge's painting, *The Uncanny Badger* (1897). Upon returning from Japan, La Farge noted: "With the Japanese the badger is uncanny. He misleads by many tricks and takes wayfarers out of the way."

The Poems of Emily Montague were inspired by a sympathetic rereading (after some twenty years) of Frances Brooke's *The History of Emily Montague*. Edited by Mary Jane Edwards. Ottawa: Carleton University Press, 1985.

The Poetry of George Jehoshaphat Mountain (1789–1863) is a response to the romanticism of Mountain's own poems and hymns, many of which were written during his long canoe trips, and later published as *Songs of the Wilderness* in 1846.

Benjamin West is drawn, to some extent, from West's most spectacular painting of the "terrible sublime," *Death on a Pale Horse* (1817).

Slumber Music draws principally upon two sources: the life and work of Henry Alline (1748–84), the Maritime preacher, hymnologist, and visionary, and an essay by M. H. Abrams, "The Correspondent Breeze: A Romantic Metaphor." In *The Correspondent Breeze: Essays on English Romanticism*. New York: W. W. Norton & Company, 1984. The title is from Samuel Taylor Coleridge's *Sibylline Leaves*:

Methinks, it should have been impossible
Not to love all things in a world so fill'd,
Where the breeze warbles and the mute still Air
Is Music slumbering on its instrument!

Captivity Voyage makes free use of Pierre-Esprit Radisson's own idiosyncratic English spelling (or that of his francophone translator/redactor). The poems are woven out of hints and nuances in his writings. I am indebted to Germaine Warkentin for an illuminating essay, "Pierre-Esprit Radisson and the Language of Place" (*Queen's Quarterly*, Volume 101, Number 2, Summer 1994). My starting point was Warkentin's observation that Radisson's genius (as self-publicist and shape-changer) was "his ability to believe absolutely in the moment in which he was living."

Pᴀᴅᴅʏ McCᴀʟʟᴜᴍ's poems have been published in *Arc, Grain, Canadian Literature, Prism international, Descant, The Dalhousie Review, Event, Queen's Quarterly, The Malahat Review, The New Quarterly*, and *The Fiddlehead*. His work has also appeared in the anthology *On the Threshold: Writing Toward the Year 2000* (Beach Holme). Recently he won the *Arc* Millennium Poetry Prize. He lives in Gibsons, British Columbia.